TEACHERS' CHOICES

Logo Illustration by Chris Van Allsburg

ENTRY

Counting and Numbers

by Sheila Cato
illustrations by Sami Sweeten

Carolrhoda Books, Inc./Minneapolis

This edition published in 1999 by Carolrhoda Books, Inc.

Carolrhoda Books, Inc., c/o The Lerner Publishing Group
241 First Avenue North, Minneapolis, MN 55401 U.S.A.

Website address: www. lernerbooks.com

LIBRARY OF CONGRESS CATALOGING-IN-PUBLICATION DATA
Cato, Sheila
    Counting and numbers / by Sheila Cato : illustrations by Sami Sweeten.
        p.   cm. — (A question of math book)
    Summary: A group of children introduce the concept of counting and various systems of numbering, using everyday examples and practice problems.
    ISBN 1-57505-322-5 (alk. paper)
    1. Counting—Juvenile literature. 2. Mathematics—Juvenile literature. [1. Counting. 2. Mathematics.]   I. Sweeten, Sami, ill. II. Title. III. Series: Cato, Sheila, 1936-   Question of math book.
QA113.C39 1999
513.2'11—dc21   98-15724

The series A Question of Math is produced by Carolrhoda Books, Inc., in cooperation with Brown Packaging Partworks Limited, London, England. The series is based on a concept by Sidney Rosen, Ph.D.
Series consultant: Kimi Hosoume, University of California at Berkeley
Editor: Anne O'Daly
Designers: Janelle Barker and Duncan Brown

Printed in Singapore
Bound in the United States of America

1 2 3 4 5 6 - JR - 04 03 02 01 00 99

Here is Brad with his number friend, Digit. Brad is learning about math the fun way by solving some number problems. Digit is going to help him. You can join in too. You will need a paintbrush, some paint, a book, some squared paper, two dice, and a pack of playing cards. Have fun!

I know the order of numbers from 1 to 10. I need to practice putting the numbers from 11 to 20 in the right order. Can you think of a fun way to do this?

I'm sure I can help you, Brad. Here's a box of number buttons. Find the button with 11 on it. Pin the button on your T-shirt.

Order Of Numbers

We do many things in order. We brush our teeth after we eat, not before. When we count, we do it in a special order, too.

Now pin the button with 12 on it next to 11.
13 comes next, then 14, and 15.
Keep doing this until you get to 20.

Thanks, Digit. And I can practice saying the numbers 11 to 20 while I am wearing my T-shirt.

Now You Try

Put these things in the right order – putting on shoes, fastening shoes, walking to school, putting on socks.

At the swimming pool, our team came 1st in one race and 3rd in another race. What is this kind of number called?

That's a good question. Numbers like 1st, 2nd, 3rd, and 4th are called *ordinal* numbers. Ordinal numbers tell you the order of things.

Putting on socks, putting on shoes, fastening shoes, walking to school

Look at your number buttons again.
The 11 button is 1st in the line.
The 12 button is 2nd. Which buttons
are the 4th and the 7th?

**The 4th button has the number 14 on it.
The 7th button has 17 on it.**

So the ordinal number of the 14 button
is 4th, and the ordinal number of
the 17 button is 7th.

Cardinal and Ordinal

The *cardinal*
number tells
you how many
things there are
in a group.
The *ordinal*
number tells you
which order the
things are in.

Now You Try

Make a list
of the days
of the
week with
Sunday as
the 1st day.
Which is the
5th day?

Look at this old clock! I know how to tell time, but I've never seen letters on a clock before. What are they called?

Those letters are called Roman numerals. They were invented by people who lived hundreds of years ago in a place called Rome. You sometimes see Roman numerals on clocks and watches. The letter I stands for the number 1. The letter V is 5. X is 10. Look at the clock face and see if you can figure out how the Romans counted.

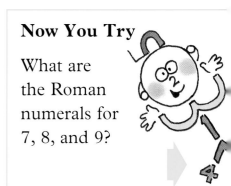

Roman Numerals

This way of counting is very old. But you can still see Roman numerals on watches and on big clocks on town and city buildings. Next time you look at a clock, see what kind of numbers it has on it.

I can see that I is at 1 o'clock. II is at 2 o'clock, and III is at 3 o'clock. IV is at 4 o'clock.

That's very good. Remember I told you that V is 5? Well, IV means "1 less than 5." And VI means "1 more than 5," so VI is the Roman numeral for 6.

Now I know how to count like an ancient Roman!

Now You Try

What are the Roman numerals for 7, 8, and 9?

9

Chinese people have an interesting way of counting. Can you please explain it, Digit?

Chinese numbers are very different from the ones we use. In the picture, the first row is the numbers 1 to 5. The second row is the numbers 6 to 10.

Can you see that the numbers are made from 10 different symbols? The numbers 11 to 20 are made by putting two symbols together.

Our counting system uses 10 symbols, too!

Counting Symbols

Our counting system has 10 symbols – 0, 1, 2, 3, 4, 5, 6, 7, 8, and 9. We call them digits. All the numbers you can think of are made of these digits.

1	一
2	二
3	三
4	四
5	五
6	六
7	七
8	八
9	九
10	十
11	十一
12	十二
13	十三
14	十四
15	十五
16	十六
17	十七
18	十八
19	十九
20	二十

Now You Try

Use a fine paintbrush and some black paint. Practice painting the Chinese numerals in the picture. Can you paint your age?

I know that if we divide a candy bar into 4 equal pieces, each part is a quarter. What is each part called if we divide the bar into 3 or 5 equal pieces?

You know, Brad, that a quarter is written like this: ¼. The 4 underneath the line tells you that you have divided one whole unit into 4 equal parts. The 1 above the line tells you that you have 1 of those parts.

Fractions

If you divide a whole unit into equal pieces, each piece is the same fraction.

If you divide the bar into 3 equal parts, each part is called a third. We write it like this: $\frac{1}{3}$. If you break the bar into 5 equal parts, each piece is called a fifth. We write it like this: $\frac{1}{5}$.

Now You Try

If Brad shared his candy bar with Luis, and each piece was the same size, what would each piece be called?

13

My brother and my grandfather have their birthdays on the same day. I'm making birthday cards for them by cutting out digits and sticking them on some paper. My brother will be 16 and my grandfather will be 61. Why is the order of numbers important?

It's easy, Brad. When there is more than one digit in a number, the value of each digit depends on where it is. Each digit tells you how many units, tens, and hundreds there are in the number.

Each piece is ½ or a half

14

Let's think about the digits on your brother's card. The 1 means 1 ten and the 6 means 6 units. The total value of the number is 16.

So on my grandfather's card, the 6 means 6 tens and the 1 means 1 unit. That makes 61. I can see that the order is really important. I'd better not get the cards mixed up!

Place value

The number 111 has one hundred, one ten, and one unit. In this number, the digit 1 has three different values.

Now You Try

Write the number that has 1 in the hundreds place, 4 in the tens place, and 8 in the units place.

15

At the basketball game, the home team scored 0, or nothing. Is 0 a real number?

Yes, Brad, it is. 0 is an important digit in our number system because it is a place holder. Sometimes it goes into the space between other numbers.

148

16

When we have a number like 104, the 1 tells us we have one hundred, the 0 tells us there are no tens, and the 4 tells us we have 4 units.

I can see that 0 is a special number. We couldn't manage without it.

Working with 0

If we add 0 to a number, the number stays the same. If we subtract 0 from a number, the number stays the same. Multiplying a number by 0 always has the answer 0.

Now You Try

What is the value of 0 in the number 4,025? 4 is 4 thousands, 2 is 2 tens, and 5 is 5 units.

Luis and I have been given a jar of jellybeans. We want to know how many jellybeans there are in the jar. We've guessed 130. Is there an easy way to find out if we are right?

It can be very hard to count when there are lots of things. Guessing is a good idea. Here's a way to check your guess. Pour half the jellybeans onto a plate and count them. That way, you can see how close your guess was to the right answer.

There were 48 jellybeans in half the jar. We have changed our guess to 100 jellybeans all together. Let's keep counting and see what we find.

Now you have counted all the jellybeans. There are 104 jellybeans in the jar. You can see that your first guess was a lot more than the total number. But by counting half the jellybeans and then guessing again, you got closer to the answer.

Guessing

Sometimes there are too many things to count, like the number of people at a baseball game. We have to guess the number.

Now You Try

Guess how many words there are on this page. Then count them to see how close you were to the right answer.

When we play baseball, the umpire writes down the score using tiny lines. Why does he count like this?

This is called tallying. The umpire needs to watch the game at the same time as he keeps the score. He needs a quick and easy way of counting.

117 words

Each of the tiny lines is a one. The score is written in groups of 5.

1, 2, 3, and 4 are marked as small lines going down.

When the umpire reaches 5, he draws a line across the 4 up-and-down lines.

Then when the game is over, he counts the score in groups of 5.

Now I know why the umpire adds the numbers together at the end of the game before he tells us who has won.

Tallying

This quick way of counting is used when there is no time to write down digits and numbers. Try using it yourself!

Now You Try

Get one of your favorite books and choose one page. Make a tally of how many times the word "the" is used. Now ask a friend to do the same thing. Do you both get the same answer?

We've made a list of all the pets belonging to the children in our class. There are 8 dogs, 10 cats, 1 rabbit, 3 birds, and 4 mice. How can we show this?

You could draw a bar graph. It's best to use some graph paper to do this. Draw a line across the bottom. This will tell you what kinds of pets your classmates have. The line going up tells you the number of each pet.

Color in the squares to show how many pets there are. There are 8 dogs, so color in 8 squares in the dog column. There are 10 cats, so color 10 squares in the cat column. I'll leave you to do the rest.

This is a great way to show how many pets we have. It's just like looking at a picture.

Now You Try

How many pets do the children in the class have all together?

Mia, Holly, Josh, and I have made some cookies. Some have cherries in them, some have raisins, others have nuts, and the rest have chocolate chips. All the cookies are mixed up on the cooling rack. We need to sort them so that we can count how many we have of each.

That will be easy. The cherry cookies are round, the raisin cookies are square, the nut cookies are star-shaped, and the chocolate chip cookies are triangles. Take all the round cookies and put them on one plate. Now take all the square cookies and put them on another plate.

There are 26 pets

I'll leave you to sort out the rest of the cookies. Now you can count how many of each type of cookie you have made.

There are 3 cherry cookies, 5 raisin cookies, 6 nut cookies, and 8 chocolate chip cookies. It was much easier to count them after we had sorted them into groups.

Sorting into Groups

Lots of things are sorted into groups. Children are put into groups for school classes and for team games. Books are put into groups in a library to make it easier to find what you are looking for.

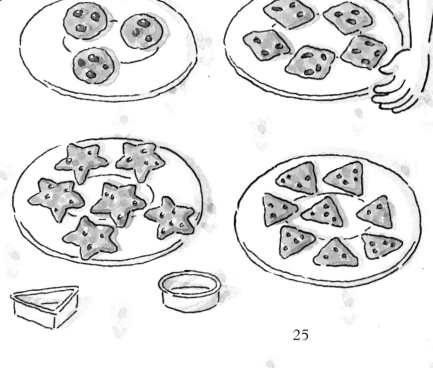

Now You Try

Make a bar graph showing the number of each group of cookies.

I'm keeping a diary this week to show what I do each day. Is there a way to show how many hours I spend on each activity?

The best way to show this is to draw a pie chart.

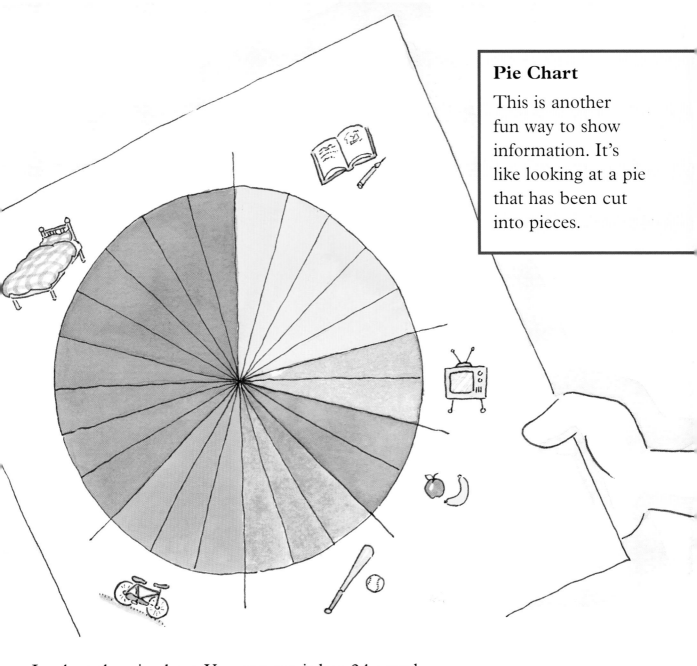

Pie Chart

This is another fun way to show information. It's like looking at a pie that has been cut into pieces.

Look at the pie chart. You can see it has 24 equal parts, one for each hour of the day. This is the pie chart for Monday. You spent 5 hours at school, 2 hours watching TV, 3 hours on your bike, 2 hours eating, and 9 hours sleeping. How many hours did you spend playing baseball?

That's easy, Digit. I spent 3 hours playing. I like this way of showing what I did on Monday.

Now You Try

Use the pie chart to find out how many hours Brad was awake.

I know I have to learn how to count, but why are numbers so important?

Numbers are everywhere. Just look around you. There are numbers on a clock face, on the pages of a book, on the calendar, on a thermometer, and lots of other places too.

15 hours

28

Numbers Everywhere

Numbers are all around us – at home, at school, in the shops. There are numbers on houses, streets, trains, clocks, and calendars.

Think about all the things you did today that used numbers.

Well, I called Holly, so I had to dial her phone number. I wrote in my diary, so I had to look at the date. I went to the store to buy some candy, so I looked at the price tag. I delivered newspapers, so I had to check the numbers on the houses.

Now You Try

Make a list of all the times you use numbers during the day.

I like to play games with my friends.
It helps us practice what we have learned.
Do you know any number games, Digit?

Here's a game called twin dice. You need two dice,
and two or more people can play. Think of a number
that comes after 3 and before 11. Take turns to
throw the dice. Add the numbers that have been thrown.
If the numbers add up to the number you chose, shout
out the number as loud as you can!

Number Games

Number games are a fun way to learn about numbers and counting. You can use dice or playing cards, or you can even make your own number cards. See if you can think of any other games.

This game is called count-a-card. You can play it with Mia. You will need a pack of playing cards. Take out all the kings, queens, and jacks. (These are the cards with pictures on them.) Give half the pack to Mia. Now, think of a number between 4 and 19.

Turn your top card face up and put it on a pile. Mia turns her top card face up and starts another pile. Keep on adding cards to the piles. When the cards on top of the piles add up to the number you chose, shout out the number. The person who shouts first wins 1 point. Keep on playing until one of you has 5 points.

Numbers are everywhere. I know about Roman numerals and Chinese numbers. I can record numbers quickly by tallying, and I can guess when there are too many things to count. I have learned how to draw a bar graph and a pie chart. I know about fractions and zero. Learning about numbers is fun, and I can even play number games with my friends!

Here are some useful number words

Cardinal numbers: Cardinal numbers tell you how many things there are in a group.

Even numbers: Even numbers end in 2, 4, 6, 8, or 0.

Fractions: When we divided a whole unit into equal parts, the pieces are called fractions.

Odd numbers: Odd numbers end in 1, 3, 5, 7, or 9.

Ordinal numbers: Ordinal numbers tell you about the order of things.

Tallying: Tallying is a quick way to show numbers.